The Practice of Recollection

A GUIDE TO BUDDHIST MEDITATION

Bhikkhu Mangalo

1978

Prajñā Press

Boulder

Prajñā Press
Great Eastern Book Company
P.O. Box 271
Boulder, Colorado 80306

ISBN 0-87773-704-5

Printed in the United States of America

The photograph on the cover is a glazed pottery statue of a Lohan, made during the Liao-Chin Dynasty (10th-13th century) in China. The photograph is reproduced courtesy of the Nelson Gallery-Atkins Museum, Kansas City, Missouri (Nelson Fund).

FOREWORD

The Practice of Recollection (*Satipatthāna*) is one of the basic practices of Buddhism.

Buddhism is rightly famous amongst the family of religions for its clarity and its undogmatic, practical approach to the question of the realisation of the Truth. It is not surprising therefore that we find right at the heart of Buddhism a stress on the need for training the mind to a greater awareness and clarity. This is done by the simple, yet eminently reasonable and practical expedient of keeping the mind focused on the present, on what *is*, here and now. But this is already more than a simple matter of mind-training or an expedient in the sense of a "device", since, as the Truth *is* what *is*, it is by keeping the mind thus trained on the simple present before us (without the smoke screen of preferences and associated thoughts, through which we see not what *is*, but what we think *about* it), that we find that this awareness is the simple and direct "door to the Deathless"— to the direct realisation of the Unborn, and therefore Undying Reality that is always with us, at the heart of our Being, hidden by the veil of ignorant thoughts.

The modern world is clearly thirsting for a new, undogmatic, scientific and practical approach to the realisation of the perennial truths that everyone instinctively knows exist—but which he feels are obscured from his direct, personal grasp by organised dogmatic "religion". Thus, in the end, even the word "religion" comes to acquire, in the minds of some people, a pejorative association, which is a pity, as they then turn in despair from "religion", seeking truths to which only religion—in the true sense—can afford them access. This thirst for an undogmatic and practical approach can be satisfied by the simple Practice of Recollection, which is, indeed, "the heart of Buddhist meditation".

The practice of recollection has the added advantage that, once one has acquired the habit, it can and indeed *should* be practised at all times and throughout the day, whatever one's occupation. It is not an exercise of "meditation" limited to formal "sittings". It is, more truly, a new way of life, a heightened state of awareness, in which, by virtue of staying in the present, instead of in the scotch mist of fantasies, life is lived more abundantly. Far from interfering with one's work and the functions of daily life, the peace and clear awareness it brings render one correspondingly more master of oneself and more clear-headed in one's judgment. This is one of the greatest glories of this practice—that it *is* applicable at *all* times, and in all situations.

Strictly speaking Recollection is not the exclusive property of Buddhism. It is the essence of the spiritual life, and wherever religion has been taken to its highest level, as a "full-time job" amongst the truly dedicated of all religions, one comes across the Practice of Recollection. The alternative is Forgetfulness and the blind, impulse-driven, semi-animal life this entails. The name Recollection may vary. It may be called mindfulness, the guarding of the heart, attention, sobriety, restraint of the senses, living in samadhi, mauna, silence of the heart, hesychasm (meaning rest), emptiness, holy indifference, equanimity, samatha and vipassana, the samadhi of prajñā, acittata, unsupported thought, dying to the ego, the elimination of conceptual thought, in the seeing to see only what is seen (*ditthe ditthamattam*), and a host of other names. As the "Practice of the Presence of God" it comes to the same, since it is only constant Recollection that can establish the mind in the awareness "It is the will of God acting through me—I am only the instrument". The Hua Ton practice of Zen, or Ramana Maharshi's method of enquiring "Who am I?"—all are Recollection, since it is this function which sees each thought as it arises, before it follows into the stream of associations, and by Recollection one comes to see "whence" it has come and "where" it returns—one comes to realise that which neither arises nor passes. It is for this reason that the Buddha described Recollection as the "Only Way", and, while promising "Recollection leads to the Deathless", warned "Forgetfulness is Death".

Though thus by no means the sole prerogative of "Buddhism", nonetheless it is in the teachings of the Buddha that the Practice of Recollection is given its greatest emphasis, as well as the clearest descriptions of *how* to put it into practice. It is one thing to come across fragmentary, enigmatic references to it in the writings of an obscure mystic; it is quite another to come across clear, detailed descriptions of a practice as a central theme throughout the discourses of the supreme authority of a great religion.   This is not surprising, for if "Christianity is the most materialistic of all religions" (as the late Archbishop of Canterbury says), Buddhism can well claim to be the most practical and precise, omitting nothing of essential practical value, adding nothing of purely theoretical interest ; for the Buddha would frequently dismiss purely speculative queries as not of practical significance.   He was intent, not on teaching dogmas—however true—for the assent of faith or intellect, but on leading people, ordinary people, to a direct personal realisation of Truth for themselves.   Since, as all agree, the Ultimate Truth is beyond the intellect, he preferred to bring them face to face with that Truth, by Recollection, than to lead them up the primrose path of intellectual sophistry.

The Practice is systematically taught in the Far East, especially in Burma, where it was revived and popularised under the able and learned guidance of the Ven. Mahasi Sayadaw at Sasana Yeikta, Rangoon.   From there, interest in this ancient yet eminently modern practice has spread to many other countries.   We have confidence that those who apply it will find it indeed a most practical and simple "door to the Deathless".

> "You yourself must make the effort ;
> Buddhas do but point the Way".

January 1970

A MANUAL OF
THE PRACTICE OF RECOLLECTION

*A detailed treatment is given in the two Satipatthāna Suttas,
Digha-Nikāya 22 and Majjhima-Nikāya 10.
Digha-Nikāya (*Dialogues of the Buddha*), Vol. II
Sutta 22, Mahā Satipatthāna Suttanta.
Majjhima-Nikāya (*The Middle Length Sayings*)
Sutta 10, Satipatthānasutta
(Discourse on the Applications of Mindfulness)

THE PRACTICE OF RECOLLECTION

The Mad Monkey

The best way to start is to see where one starts from.

Let us take a look at the mind of an ordinary worldly person. What we find is a grasshopper mind, a butterfly mind, chasing its fancies and impulses of the moment, the prey of stimuli and its own emotional reaction to them—a reaction that is largely a purely conditioned and blind one. A chain of linked associations, hopes, fears, memories, fantasies, regrets, stream constantly through the mind, triggered off by momentary contact with the outside world through the senses. It is a blind, never-ceasing, never-satisfied search for satisfaction, bewildered, aimless, suffering. This is not reality, but a waking dream, a sequence of concepts and fantasies. The world is split up into recognisable identified forms, each of which has its name, and on the basis of these names—conceptual images of the reality around—the mind spins its web of thought in which it entangles itself. Objects change, but their "name" remains the same, and the mind, left clinging to empty names and images, loses touch with reality, trying to find in the products of its own imagination the satisfaction and security for which it thirsts. No wonder the mind has been called an "idol-factory", and no wonder that the Buddha described such a mind as a restless monkey swinging from branch to branch in the quest for satisfying fruit through the endless jungle of conditioned events. The futility, unreality and frustration inherent in such a mode of existence is startlingly self-apparent once one begins to see it clearly.

It is the purpose of Buddhism, and of religion in general, to re-unite one with the Reality one has thus lost sight of due to one's ignorance in seeking the happiness for which one thirsts where it is not to be found—in the shadows and illusions of one's own mind. That modern man allows his mind to continue this blind tormented rat-race in undisciplined confusion is perhaps the wonder of wonders in an age that likes to consider itself "scientific". Man has amassed a phenomenal amount of information—concepts all of it—about the forms and names that inhabit the universe, and he has harnessed and disciplined forces of nature in a way that would have staggered his forefathers. To gain electrical power he will build structures of enormous size and cost in both money and labour, damming back great rivers in mid-stream, yet still his knowledge of reality fails him, and his own nature escapes him, while he, almost unbelievably, omits to expend the slightest labour to stem and discipline his own thoughts, even when he half perceives they delude and torment him.

Down through countless generations a few, going against the stream of human patterns, have undertaken this task, often in the face of almost incredible privations and discouragement, at first blind, and often teacherless. Some broke through triumphantly, some stumbled through after great sufferings, yet all in their different languages declare a unanimous find—there is a "something", by knowing which one knows all. It is the Uncreated, the only lasting Reality ; it is our own true Being, and its "discovery" is, all are agreed, the supreme happiness, beside which all the suffering of ages is suddenly quite insignificant. And in some strange yet certain way, those who find It find the Deathless, they step outside of both birth and death. This is beyond the senses, though in it resides the power by, and in which, we see and hear and think. It is veiled by the flow of ignorant thoughts, by which we see not what is, but what we think about it. It is the old story of the man who seeing a piece of rope hanging from a tree in the twilight, mistakes it for a snake and is panicked.

So it goes on. Taking our own thoughts, mere images of reality, for reality, we allow the emotions to be aroused by them. These emotions produce more thoughts in the desire to satisfy this disturbance, and the vicious circle is complete. Without ignorance of reality one would not think about it, without the stream of thoughts there would be no distressing emotions, the mind would be at peace, and then there would be no *need* to think.

The stopping of Conceptual Thought

The first step, therefore, is to cut off the chain of associated concepts and words that flood the mind, holding it with Recollection on the present, on what *is*. Thus in a famous verse, the Buddha used to say,

> "Don't chase after the past,
> Don't seek the future ;
> The past is gone
> The future hasn't come
> But see clearly on the spot
> That object which *is now*,
> While finding and living in
> A still, unmoving state of mind".

This is the beginning of mental discipline, and the *remembering* to do so is Recollection. Without this Recollection the stream of thoughts takes over again, agitating, distressing and befouling the mind like muddy water in a lake on which the wind is blowing up waves. Clarity of vision, peace of mind and self-recollection are lost in a single instant. It is for this reason that the Buddha called Recollection "The Only Way". Or as he vividly described it by a metaphor,

> "Whatever streams flow in the world,
> Recollection is their damming-back".

As it is said in Zen, "The mad mind does not halt ; if it halts it is Enlightenment".

The practice of Recollection is a gradual training. Perfection of self-recollection is the "Art of Arts and the Science of Sciences" to which a due apprenticeship is necessary. To train one's own mind, "ours" as it is, is even harder than training a dog or horse, for the mind is no less headstrong, and has all the ingenuity and trickery of man to help it find ways to break loose. Yet this is a far more worthwhile training, bringing already in early stages great peace and joy, and in its train innumerable riches. With an unrecollected, self-willed mind there is little hope of happiness—even the simple happiness of a peaceful, purposeful and balanced life, how much less the supreme goal of life.

What then is the "practice" of Recollection ?   How does one go about it ?

Recollection is, quite simply, remembering to establish the attention with full awareness on the present, on the here and now.   It is the "unsupported thought", the "fast of the mind", the true "Aryan silence".   As each object arises into consciousness, through whichever of the six entrances (the five senses and the imagination), it must be seen *as it is*, without welcoming it or rejecting it, without clinging to it or trying to push it aside—just "letting it go as though it were a piece of rotten wood", as the great Huang Po puts it.   This is the real meaning of the "Middle Way" of Buddhism, to see each (and every) object as it arises, with a mind that is "alert, fully-conscious and self-recollected, avoiding either attachment or aversion to anything".   "Do not like, do not dislike, all will then be clear".   The Buddha used to define recollection and full consciousness as "seeing the arising, presence and passing of all perceptions, feelings and thoughts".   He often used to say that his teaching 'in brief' was "To see only the seen in what is seen ; and in the heard to hear only what is heard".   It is all the same.

But when we try to *do* this, what do we find ?   We find that, at first, to do so for even a few minutes is quite impossible ; the mind is swept away by a stream of erupting thoughts (*āsavā*) and a restlessness that makes it quite impossible to be clear and detailed enough to avoid reacting to the thoughts and objects that arise.   One just cannot begin.   It is for this reason that the Buddha, in his wisdom, compassion and "skill in means", taught the Practice of Recollection as a gradual method of training, whereby, from the initial chaos and confusion of an undisciplined, wild-bull mind, the mind can be weaned from "whoring after strange gods", to be still and know THAT WHICH IS.

The Foundations of Recollection

First, though, a word of warning.   Proper "Samādhi" or stillness of mind, the last step on the Buddha's Noble Eightfold Path leading to Realisation, is only possible with proper Recollection, the step before it.   Similarly this Recollection is dependent on the steps preceding it, which comprise, in brief, Right Understanding, morality and determination. There must be at least a good foundation of understanding to realise the futility of the transient and conditioned in the light of the Unconditioned—and of all objects—when one is looking for "*me*", the subject. Else the mind will not be able to detach itself enough from thinking about the ever-changing objects, so as to practise poised self-recollection in the here and now. It will want to be off thinking of its "idols", for where one's treasure (*ratanā*) is, there will one's heart (*citta*) be also. Similarly, without at least a good foundation on a moral attitude to life, Recollection is being built on sand. An evil conscience is indeed like muddied water in which nothing can be seen clearly "as it is". Without peace of mind there is little hope of stemming the flow of thoughts, not with all the determination in the world—even so it is hard enough. Of course none of us is perfect—far from it—and we all fail to live up to what we know we should be, but without at least a sincere and manful effort to put the basic Buddhist precepts into practice, one is just accelerating and braking at the same time. Later, increased self-awareness and peace will bring greater self-control, but at least the sincere *will* and effort to goodness must be there, and a sincere regret (and if possible restitution) for any evil done.

Above all the mind must be starting to turn away from the old patterns, which is the true meaning of "repentance"—metanoia.

Taking a Course of Recollection

The best way to learn the Practice of Recollection is to take a "course" under a competent instructor, putting oneself unreservedly in his hands, and doing the practice exactly as he indicates. These instructions, in this case, are meant only as a basic guide and reference when the use of such is felt necessary—and for those who, for any reason, find themselves unable to do the practice under an instructor, but who wish nonetheless to make a start for themselves.

With an instructor the difficulties are greatly reduced as he will be able to keep a check on progress by daily "reports", and to correct any dangers of an incorrect application of the principles of the practice. It also is found to be a great help to the feeling of confidence, both in the practice and in oneself, to do it—at least for a period—under guidance. Many people find that their daily interview with their instructor, apart from ironing out specific difficulties, acts as a sort of "recharge" of their inspiration and determination batteries. To *feel* that things are not going too well is not necessarily a proof that they are *not* doing so. Indeed, it can even be a sign of progress, as at last one is beginning to see just how badly one has been doing the practice. In other words, one is beginning to see things much more clearly at last. Nonetheless, subjectively one may not be aware of this at the time, and it can be a great boost to one's energies after dejectedly painting a black picture to one's instructor of how unable one is to control the mind, to see him smile with pleasure and satisfaction, and say, almost rubbing his hands, "Ah, now things are really looking-up !"—and to see that he really means it ! From his experience, he will be able to tell just how things are going, often by apparently insignificant little details. The best thing, therefore, is to trust his experience and judgement, and telling him all the details of how things are going, leave it to him to gauge how, in fact, they *have* been going. The continual "running commentary" entailed in assessing one's own progress all the time is a great hindrance to true progress. Some people have a tendency to tell their instructor only what they would *like* to have happened during their practice, omitting the details of difficulties and failures they consider *should not* have been present— usually out of pride, and the attempt to deceive him that things have been going better than they have—glossing over their weaknesses. This is not wise. The instructor needs to know about the bad as well as the good sides of the practice, and *he* is the best judge of what is or is not important. Often seemingly quite insignificant details are of importance to him in gauging the progress of the practicant.

Another prevalent weakness of Westerners in practising meditation under an instructor is the desire to know far more about the "theory" side, and "what is going on", than is either necessary or skilful. Thus they are often full of innumerable unnecessary questions and objections that only spring from and cause more *thoughts*—and thinking is, as we have seen, the opposite of the Practice of Recollection. Theory should be left aside for the time being. The best thing is just to do as the instructor advises. Like the umpire, his decision should be taken as final.

Related to this question is the Westerner's preoccupation with the concepts of psychology—"making the unconscious conscious" and the like, so that he even starts to *look* for "upsurges from the unconscious", "problems presenting themselves for solution" and so forth. It should be impressed most firmly that psychological analysis is not a part of the Practice of Recollection, the sole purpose of which is to see more clearly, *without thinking discursively about it*, what *is*, at each moment, *now* in the present. Analysis deals with concepts. Meditation aims at stilling the mind and watching what *is*, dispassionately. No thoughts—no "me", no "me"—no neurosis. Just, moreover, as the mind refreshes itself in sleep, or when by occupational therapy it is kept off its preoccupations, and just as a cut in one's finger if cleaned and left to rest is cured by "nature", so the mind will best cure itself by rest, and by being kept clean, clean of emotional stimulants and harassing preoccupations. Nothing effects this so well as the practice of Recollection. If one perseveres in the practice, moreover, one comes more and more to see the unreality of the "me" concept, which cuts the foundation away from all mental illness and distress. No device or way of looking at things, and no amount of "making the unconscious conscious" will deliver one from (for example) "insecurity", so long as it is for "me", this body and mind, that one is seeking security. They *are* impermanent, and no juggling will alter that fact or lend them a false security. Once the idea of "me" in the body drops out, the whole problem drops out with it. For this reason, during the Practice of Recollection at least, psychological analysis is best put aside. The "me" thought itself is the problem—not its preoccupations, nor the forms it takes.

The Western need to intellectualise over one's own meditational practice is one of the main reasons why Westerners usually find it much harder, and take much longer, to complete a course of meditation than do their Eastern equivalents. Many Easterners, by simply and conscientiously getting down to it in accordance with their instructor's guidance, will complete a course inside a few weeks. Most Westerners tend to take at least double the time.

Preliminary Steps for the Practice of Recollection

Particularly for those who are embarking on a period of full-scale Practice of Recollection in a course, it is wise to arrange that the time during one's practice will not be interrupted. The ideal is that one should undertake a full course under instruction for an *indefinite period* of time, in other words until the instructor is satisfied that the full benefits of the course have been gained. Otherwise, thoughts about the approaching time of departure, and the feeling of needing to get it finished by then, can be a serious harassment to the meditator.

In practice, however, such an indefinite period is not always feasible, especially in the unfavourable conditions of Western culture and its wage-earning commitments. Still, even a limited time will pay its dividends if undertaken resolutely and in the right spirit ; and at least a minimum period should be put aside, and no further thoughts of "how much longer shall I go on for ?" indulged in. So far as is possible, too, one should try to dispose of the necessary activities which might otherwise cause distraction, things like letter-writing, shopping, business and financial preoccupations, family worries and the like. For the duration of the period of meditation one should try to lay aside all thoughts of all subjects not directly concerned with the meditation, i.e. with the here and now.

During the period of meditation, moreover, one should try to keep one's life as simple as possible, cutting out unnecessary frills and fancies. To spend hours daily on clothes, food and drink is not conducive to good meditation. Indeed most meditators would be wise to undertake the Eight Precepts which Eastern Buddhists traditionally do during periods of meditation. These entail (at least temporary) renunciation of such things as dressing for show, cosmetics, entertainments and "amusements". The idea of dressing up for "morale", if clearly seen, is a fine example of the devices the mind uses to find a spurious feeling of security, and to convince us what nice, attractive people we are. Even without such distractions the mind will be restless enough and, particularly at times, will be only too eager to find *anything* to do rather than do what seems to be "nothing". The future is best left to the future. (It probably won't happen anyway !) The past is best left to the past. (The mind is very selective about what it cares to remember from the past). Similarly one should try to avoid all unnecessary talk, writing, reading, and gadding about. A good motto to take for the period of practice is "Eat less, sleep less, talk less—meditate more". Particularly after the first few days of the Practice of Recollection, it should be found that considerably less sleep is necessary. It is the brain which uses the greater part of oxygen in the blood, which it burns up in emotional energy and tensions which harass and distress us, both mentally and physically. All this is due to the amount of emotionally tinged thought-weaving the mind is usually (though not "naturally") engaged in. When this is cut down by a greater self-awareness in the Practice of Recollection, the resultant peace and freedom from the constant petty-emotionalism means that far less recuperation is needed—the mind is already being rested and healed—and therefore far less sleep is necessary. Indeed it is the general rule for serious practitioners of Recollection (for example in the meditation monasteries in the East) to be able to cut down quickly to four hours sleep a night, and before long to about two. Eventually it is even very common for them to spend days, even weeks altogether without sleep, in twenty-four hours of unbroken meditation, not only without tiredness or ill-effects, but, indeed, with a positive sense of well-being and hitherto unknown clarity and peace of mind.

To achieve this sort of state, however, demands a real dedication to the practice, at least for the period for which it has been undertaken. If this is forthcoming, all of this and much more will be experienced for oneself, and be still compatible with being a "man of the world", with a job to do, a family to go back to, and functions in life to fulfil.

Above all, though, one should try to keep one's life simple, to avoid unnecessary conversations with everyone except one's instructor, and all reading. These external conversations will tend to prolong themselves afterwards in the form of internal imaginary conversations, which is all that thought is, anyway.

Basic Breathing Exercise

With these preliminaries, and the right general attitude of mind, the best way to start the practice of Recollection is, as the Buddha clearly describes in the "Discourse on the Practice of Recollection" (*Satipatthāna-sutta*), to sit down and establish the attention on the one most visible constant function of the body—the breathing. This is a semi-automatic function (*sankhāra*) that is always present with us in normal life, and which is emotionally quite neutral. For these reasons it is the ideal object of use for learning to become recollected, and to hold one's attention on what is going on *now*, in the present, and *here*, *in* us. Most people agree that in practice (theoretical considerations quite apart) the most conducive position to sit in, if one can manage it, is cross-legged. This need not be in the famous "full lotus" position, with the feet lifted back up on to the opposite thigh, nor even in the "half-lotus" position—which can cause many people almost as much pain as a "half-nelson". The simple "easy" posture, with the legs just placed cross-wise on the floor is quite sufficient, and if necessary a strategic cushion can be placed under a troublesome knee. If sitting cross-legged is not convenient, however, it is of no great importance. Nowadays even many meditation instructors in the East do their meditation sitting in a chair. The only important considerations are that one should have an alert, upright, perfectly straight-backed posture which can be held without indescribable agony for a minimum of one hour or so. While doing the practice one should be sitting still (without fidgeting) and relaxed but alert, with the hands either in the usual position to be seen in statuettes of the Buddha in meditation, or simply lying lightly cupped one inside the other. The head should be held upright, the eyes closed, and all muscles, in so far as is possible, relaxed and easy. Once taken up, one should try to avoid unnecessary readjusting of the posture for the given period.

The proper place to concentrate the attention on the breathing is at the face wherever it is most prominent. This varies slightly from person to person. Some find the best spot is just above the upper lip, others just at the tip of the nose, others again on the inside of the nostrils. It is immaterial. What is important is that it should be wherever one, oneself, finds it most clear. A few experimental breaths should soon establish that. The attention should be on the *physical sensation* of the touch of the air, not the *concept* of breathing. Nor should the breathing be interfered with or deliberately regulated. At first, this may be a little difficult, and in the preliminary stages it is not easy to dissociate *pure attention* from *control*. However, in that case one should just try to avoid unnecessary and unnatural control of the breath in any way, and just breathe easily, naturally and at a normal rhythm, but with the mind held on the sensation of the touch of the air. At first, too, it may well be found difficult to catch this touch of air clearly. Press on regardless. Practice and persistence will greatly improve this. One should try, moreover, to be aware of the sensation of the breath from the time it starts the inbreath until it stops, and then, again, from the start of the outbreath to its end. As one breathes in one should repeat "In", and as one breathes out one should repeat "Out". This is a check to see that the mind is really doing the practice and not wandering.

Before he has been going on with the practice for very long, the beginner will find a constant tendency for the mind to be torn away from the observation of the breathing. Thoughts and memories of the past, hopes and fears for the future, imaginations, fantasies, intellectualisations on theory, doubts and worries about one's meditation, pictures and shapes in front of the mind's eye, and distracting external stimuli such as noises, pains, itches, impulses to move etc., all tend perpetually to beckon the mind aside into "interesting sidelines". There is no need to be unduly upset or discouraged by this. After all, it is the state of mind to which one has been long accustomed. Discipline has only just begun. Rome was not built in a day. Indeed, if it were so easy as all that to govern the mind, enlightened men would be a penny-a-dozen. The Buddha has pointed out that the mind, when one starts to try to withdraw it from its evil resorts, is like a fish taken from its native water and lying thrashing on the bank. Here we have it in practice—but everyone finds, or has found, the same problem. Enlightened men are made from those who do not despair, but persevere in keeping bringing the mind back to heel, just as one does with an over-exuberant puppy one is patiently but firmly training to obedience. Here, as everywhere, one should try to take the razor's edge of the Middle Way. There should be the determination to press on—but a *calm* determination—not the sort that moves in fits and starts between the poles of despair and fanaticism. This merely shows an over-strong ego involved in the question ("*I* want to be a good meditator"). A relaxed determination is what is needed—or as the classic Buddhist commentators describe it, the perfect balance between peace (*samādhi*) and energy (*viriya*). These two, like discrimination (*paññā*) and faith (*saddhā*), should be perfectly in balance.

The way to deal with these distractions is to notice immediately, or at least as soon as possible, the fact of distraction, identifying it with an appropriate word, such as "Thinking", "Seeing", "Hearing", "Pain", "Itching", or "Impulse". Then the mind should revert to its proper activity—noting the sensation of the breath with "In" and "Out" until the next interruption, which should be dealt with in exactly the same manner. If there is any feeling of irritation at the distraction, this too should be noted as "Irritation", clearly pinpointing the sensation involved, and then the mind should revert to the breathing again. Similarly any amusement—or, for instance, pleasure at the speed with which one felt one had caught and registered a centrifugal movement of the mind—should be noted as "amusement" or "pleasure" and, again back to the breath. All such tendencies to wander should be noted as soon as possible after they have arisen—when one is more practised one can even catch them *before* they arise, by the feel of the mind starting to turn—but one should not *jump* at them, or jerk the mind in so doing. The noting should be done neither too fast nor too slowly—the middle way, that is—immediately, firmly and clearly, but not over-hurriedly. This only further agitates and distracts the mind.

It has been well said, "There is no need to be afraid of rising thoughts, but only of the delay in becoming aware of them".

If one patiently perseveres in catching the thoughts—like bringing the puppy back to heel each time he wanders—this *is* meditation, and things are going very well. What is *not* meditation is, on the one hand, to be lazy about it and sit day-dreaming, and on the other to get upset and full of despair over the feeling that the mind will just not stay put.

Another sort of thought that can be a great distraction at times are so-called "running commentary" thoughts such as, "Now I am not thinking of anything", "Things are going very well now", "This is dreadful—my mind just won't stay still"—and the like. Often these take the form of wondering what one is going to say in one's report to one's instructor, and virtually imagining the whole conversation. All such thoughts should simply be noted as "Thinking", and as Huang Po says, just "dropped like a piece of rotten wood". "Dropped" notice, not *thrown* down. A piece of rotten wood is not doing anything to irritate you, but is just of no use, so there is no point in hanging on to it. The Buddha used the same description in pointing out that all objects (*dhamma*) of the mind are not "me" or anything to do with "me"—(how could they be ? they are just *objects*, not the subject) and are, therefore, of no more significance to one than the leaves and twigs lying about on the forest ground. Why preoccupy oneself with them ? And what is the point of investigating rubbish one has only collected so as to throw away ?

In noting all such distractions, and in noting the breathing itself, the word used to note them, such as "In", "Out", or "Thinking", is purely a check that one is noting them clearly. The aim is in each case to get a clear, focused sight of the object in question. If one flips at it carelessly, with the attention out of focus, or the awareness more on the *word* than the object, one will not, obviously, see it clearly. If on the other hand one grasps at it heavy-handedly it will disturb the mind and cause more thoughts. Again, it is the middle path that is necessary.

It is for this reason that the constantly repeated "refrain" in the "Discourse on the Practice of Recollection" is that one is aware of the object with "Recollection established *just sufficiently* for clear understanding and self-recollection, while one remains unattached without grasping at anything in the world". Nor is there any need to try to retrace the links in a chain of associated thoughts, nor to try to ascertain what it was that first started the chain. Any such impulse should itself be noted simply as "Thinking", and the mind should revert to the breathing. However badly things have just been going, one should take up again at the only place one can—where one *is*, and go on from there. Psychological analyses are also "Thinking". Involuntary movements of body or limbs during the practice should also be noted in an appropriate manner as "Swaying", "Jerking", etc., then the mind should revert to the breathing.

It will normally be found that all such movements, as well as pains, itches and discomforts will cease if noted clearly and impersonally. Particularly at the beginning, however, it will sometimes be found that they do not stop immediately, but that it is necessary to notice them two or three times—sometimes more—before they eventually do give up and go away. At times, moreover, pains, itches, cramps, and the like, have a tendency to seem for a moment even to grow in intensity when pin-pointed with the attention ; but it will be found that if one continues to note them dispassionately each time the mind is drawn to them, they will eventually fade away and disappear. For this reason, even if at first a sensation seems to increase rather than to subside, one should continue to note it, with the attention clearly and unemotionally placed on the actual sensation—not the *idea* of the sensation, nor on the aversion to or fear of the pain. It will then subside and disappear. At first, though, one is not fully aware of this pattern, and when a disagreeable sensation occurs there is a subtle (sometimes not very subtle) aversion to it, and the desire to *make* it disappear. This is unskilful. The mechanism of the mind is to bring up for attention amongst all the possible objects at any given moment that particular object that it sees the mind is *interested* in ; and interest is of two sorts, for and against. To like something or to dislike it is equally a signal to the mind to bring the object up for further investigation.

That is why again, the Middle Way—between liking and disliking —is necessary. When one looks quite dispassionately, with equanimity, at whatever the mind presents, then it sees "O dear, that doesn't seem to be of interest after all ; I thought it *would* be", so to speak, and it is forced to drop the subject and move on. After all, it is the same with people. If someone comes to see you and you welcome them affectionately, they will stay for a long chat. Equally, if you greet your visitor with irritation and aversion, the chances are he will stay for a scufuffle, or at least a slanging-match. If, on the other hand, one just meets them correctly, but coolly—evidently not interested in their coming at all—they will go away.

Therefore, a genuine equanimity to the objects the mind presents will soon mean they stop coming, including such things as pains and discomforts. But mind is not mocked. The equanimity must be genuine, else it may not work immediately.

Movements

If, in the early stages, a pain or itch does not go away, even after repeated notings, but on the contrary, has grown intolerable to the point where one feels one *must* move, or scratch the offending portion of skin, one should try to notice this intention as "Intending". Then the mind should revert to the breathing again. If this pattern of noting the pain, or itch, and then the impulse to deal with it as "Intending", has been clearly followed several times till, at last, one *really must* move or scratch the itch, then noting the final "Intending", one should clearly and recollectively make the necessary movement, noting all the details involved with the apposite terms. If, for example, an itch on the forehead has reached martyring proportions, and repeated impulses of "Intending", to scratch at last force one to actually do so, then noting the last "Intending", one should slowly and deliberately lift the hand, noting as one does so "Lifting, lifting . . ." As the action will be done slowly the continuous movement will allow repeated noting of "Lifting, lifting, lifting . . ." to ensure that the mind really is concentrated on the actual movement. When the hand reaches the forehead the touching of the skin with the finger nail should be noted as "Touching", and the action of scratching as "Scratching, scratching . . ." When the sensation on the forehead indicates that the itch is now satisfied, it can be registered as "Satisfied", the impulse to replace the hand on the lap as "Intending", and the long trip home as "Moving, moving, moving . . ." and so on.

This description is just to give the general pattern, but in fact, once one has got some practice in the technique, one will find considerably more to notice even in an apparently simple little action like scratching one's forehead. A sound may distract one on the way up, or a thought, or one may have the attention taken by the change of pressure of the sleeve on the skin of the arm—and many other such things. If, in a moment's loss of self-recollection one starts a "blind", unregistered movement to scratch an itch—or anything else involving a movement—one should again, on recollecting oneself, see what one is about, register "Moving" or "Scratching", and carry on again from where one *is*. What is past is past, and there is nothing to be gained by shouting insults at oneself, nor by bursting into tears, even if, theoretically, an action undertaken from a blind, unregistered impulse is a sign of distraction, in other words, of failure in Recollection.

Thus the Buddha indicates in the "Discourse on the Practice of Recollection", "Whether bending one's arm or straightening it one acts with full awareness". That is what Recollection means, having one's wits about one, being with it whatever one is doing, seeing it "as it is"—not what one is *thinking about* it.

When such actions are completed the attention should again revert to the breathing. The above description of the way to undertake the scratching of an itch recollectedly is, of course, only a type. All other such actions, such as moving, if absolutely necessary, to ease a pain, swallowing, stretching the neck, straightening the back, opening or closing the eyes—in fact *all actions whatsoever*—should be dealt with in the same way. This is Recollection, the "direct" and "only" way.

Aches and Pains

At times during the practice pains, itches, aches, sensations of little pricking feelings, or as if an insect were crawling over the skin, and so forth, can become quite prominent. There is no call for worry (or interest), it is neither illness nor anything else untoward. These sensations spring from a variety of natural causes. Some are there all the time, but we are "normally" not fully aware of them. This can be seen if one watches the way "ignorant worldly people" are constantly changing position—yet barely, if at all, aware that they have done so from discomfort. So deep does "dukkha", the truth of suffering or discontent, go ! Even changing the ways one's legs are crossed sitting in the Underground is due to it. If one were quite satisfied who would want to change the "status quo" ?

Other of the sensations that tend to occur during meditation are caused by the unaccustomed prolonged periods of sitting still, while mind and muscles have still not yet come to the state of relaxation (*passadhi*) but are still somewhat tensed and fighting against themselves. Great peace of mind brings with it greater nervous and muscular relaxation, and this will soon get rid of this cause of discomfort, but for a time one must grin (recollectedly) and bear it (disinterestedly). Other sensations are, as it were, psychosomatic ; mind-produced by a mind that for probably a few score years has been used to "picking-flowers", grass-hoppering from one "interesting" topic to another, more or less irrespective of the "healthiness" or reality of the object. Unaccustomed therefore to prolonged attention to anything as unvaried and uninteresting as breathing, the mind becomes bored and restless and creates interesting diversions for its own amusement. This is "Mara", the evil one, trying to make you take an interest, or better still, give up Recollection altogether. However, as has been described, if his tricks are noted simply and unemotionally as "Itching", "Feeling", etc., he is forced to give up and go away ! Just as his three daughters were, when they tried to "tempt" the Buddha but he stolidly refused to react—one way or another.

At times, too, one may have the impression that noises, sensations and distractions in general, far from being *less* able to affect one, are *more* able to do so. Quite a small unexpected sound may cause a momentary start. Here too there is nothing to be worried about. All this is quite normal, and it is the path that all have to tread. There is often, moreover, a period when one seems even more vulnerable, more easily irritated, discouraged etc., than before. This too is natural, and is only a stage, which will soon pass if one presses on. The cause of this state of affairs is that the increasing fewness of stimuli, and the greater sharpness of focus on them, has the temporary effect sometimes of giving each stimulus a greater strength. If noted quietly in the described way, however, the effect is momentary, and it will soon pass.

If one presses on one soon comes to a state, where on the contrary, each stimulus, although seen with greater clarity, has, as it were, a shock-absorber, and things which before would probably have had one walking up the wall leave one now calmly noting "Hearing, hearing".

If while practising attention on the breathing, the mind notices imaginary shapes, colours, lights, or pictures of scenes, people's faces and so on, as if before the mind's eye, they should again simply be noted as "Seeing" without interest or aversion, and the mind allowed to return to the noting of the breathing. However beautiful the Persian carpet or kaleidoscopic pattern may seem to be, the best thing is just to note "Seeing", and pass on without picking out details. "Restraint of the senses" in Buddhism is defined as, "On seeing a visual object one does not grasp at its features or at any of its details", and the same is said for each of the senses. The order of the day in the Practice of Recollection is, "In the seen to see only what is seen" (*ditthe ditthamattam*). In other words "seeing", and pass on without dwelling on the object. When the mind dwells upon anything it is ceasing to practice Recollection. It has become the slave of the object, having sold its free birthright.

This practice of the Basic Breathing Exercise should be continued for one-hourly stretches (or for whatever period the instructor may recommend).

In between sessions the following basic walking exercise should be practised—also for hourly stretches—alternately with the breathing exercise, turn and turn about.

Basic Walking Exercise

Between sessions of the sitting practice the meditator should find a quiet stretch of ground where he can walk up and down relatively undisturbed. It need not be long. If one's room is not too small it can easily be done there, or along a corridor, garden path, or hall. It is best, for this exercise, if one walks deliberately much slower than one usually does. Something about the speed of a good slow march is ideal, but of course one should walk nonetheless in as simple and natural a manner as the speed allows. If there is any doubt on this score, one's instructor will soon give a demonstration. During this period of walking up and down, the attention should be on the move-ment of the feet and legs. One should note, as the right foot begins to rise from the ground, "Lifting" ; as it moves forward, "Moving" ; and as it places again on the ground, "Placing". Similarly for the left foot, and so on.

In exactly the same manner as during the sitting, breathing practice, all distracting thoughts or sensations should be noted in the apposite manner. If one happens to look up at something while walking one should immediately register "Looking", and revert to the movement of the feet. Looking about one and noticing the details of objects, even those on one's path, is "lust of the eyes" (*rupārāga*) and is *not* part of the practice—though registering "Looking", if one happens to have inadvertently done so, is. The rest is "interesting sidelines", Mara's bait-hook.

On reaching the end of one's path the need will arise to turn and walk in the opposite direction. One will become aware of this fact a pace or two before reaching the end. This intention to turn should be noted as "Intending". It may not always have been seen, particularly at first. It will always occur, however—without it one would not be able to turn—and since it is a thought which *is* there, it should be seen when possible and noted. This does not mean, however, that one should *try* to see it. That is in itself an intention and thought, and should be noted accordingly if it occurs. But since the intention to turn *is* there, if the recollection is strong, it *will* be seen, and can be noted. After noting the intention to turn, one should note all the other details of the thoughts and movements involved in the turn. As the last step forward is taken and one begins actually to turn the body, one should note "Turning", as the other foot raises "Lifting", "Turning", "Placing", and so on. Then as one steps out again on the return path, "Lifting", "Moving", "Placing". There is often a temptation, on coming to the end of one's "tether", to look up and glance about one for something interesting. If this undisciplined impulse occurs it should be noted as "Intending", and should the distracted glance happen to take place, it should be quietly but immediately noted as "Looking", and the attention can revert naturally to the movement of the feet again. There is no need in such cases to put the mind back on the feet ; once recollection is re-established the mind, of itself, knows what it should be about, and will turn of itself to it. The same is true at other times during the Practice of Recollection too.

It is normally best for beginners to start this walking exercise with a three-stage noting technique as indicated. "Lifting", "Moving",

"Placing". Depending on the capacity of the meditator, the instructor may recommend either less or more stages to register. At times, for instance, when for practical reasons it is not convenient to walk at the slow speed recommended, it is sufficient to notice a simple "Left, Right, Left, Right", technique. For example, when out and about away from meditational surroundings, a slow "Lifting, moving, placing", down Regent Street might draw a raised eyebrow from even the phlegmatic English. The important point is not so much how many or how few points of noting there are, but whether they *are being noted*, or whether the mind is off "wool-gathering".

During Daily Actions

These two practices of Breathing and Walking constitute the basis of the practice of Recollection as practised as a "technique", and particularly during a course, when life is organised to facilitate plenty of time being found for meditation. Nonetheless even during a meditation course, the little, every-day actions of life must still be dealt with. One must still get up and dress in the morning ; one must still wash, go to the lavatory, make one's bed, eat, stand up, sit down. During all such activities, a similar practice should be maintained. Indeed, strictly speaking, there is no essential difference between sitting doing the basic breathing exercise, and sitting eating bacon and eggs—only that what is going on during the breathing exercise is simple and regular, and therefore easier on the whole to keep check on. That is why it is chosen as the best way with which to start the practice of Recollection.

During daily actions, the same essential pattern is followed. Whatever *is* on the mind, one sees it clearly without clinging to it, without welcoming it or rejecting it, and to ensure that one is doing it properly one notes the momentary objects with an appropriate term. After long experience in the practice, even this last little check that recollection has not been lost can be dispensed with, and one just *sees* with a silent, but implicit awareness of each object. Nonetheless, this is not easy, particularly while the mind is only too eager to chase off after the shadows anyway. And until a great deal of experience and progress has been achieved in the practice of Recollection it is wiser to keep to the explicit registration of the objects in the way indicated.

It may be of interest to the meditator to see at this point the whole of the paragraph of the "Discourse on the Practice of Recollection" in which the Buddha indicates in brief how the practice should be maintained in all the smallest actions of life. It reads as follows,

"Whether going out or returning, the bhikkhu acts with full awareness ; whether looking ahead or looking round, he acts with full awareness ; whether bending (his arm) or straightening it, he acts with full awareness ; in taking his over-robe, bowl and spare under-robe, he acts with full awareness ; whether defecating or urinating, he acts with full awareness ; whether walking, standing or sitting, whether resting or awake, whether talking or silent, he acts with full awareness".

This little paragraph speaks volumes ! Short, terse and stylised as it is to facilitate memorisation, it outlines by emphasising salient features of daily life how *all* actions of life should be included—even down to answering the calls of nature—to emphasise that *nothing* is too trivial or sordid to apply Recollection to. This discourse was spoken to monks (bhikkhus), therefore their life and articles (robes and alms-bowls) are mentioned, and since the life of the Buddhist monk, theoretically at least, consisted of the simple routine of going once a day, in the early morning, to the nearest village for alms, carrying all his possessions—spare robe, bowl, needle etc., with him, returning, eating whatever had been put in his bowl, and then spending the rest of the day "walking or sitting" (*cankamena nisajjāya*) in meditation, it is not surprising that the actions and articles described here are simple. Nevertheless the Buddha did not intend this practice for monks alone, but for all who took their religion seriously. The ancient Commentary to this Discourse describes how even some of the village women going to draw water from the village well would do so practising Recollection.

In applying the practice of Recollection during these small actions, it is best if the action is done as slowly and deliberately as possible so as to enable the action to be noted clearly in all its details, without flurrying the mind, which would only cause distraction, and the arising of associated thoughts. If practised properly Recollection leads directly to stillness of mind (*samādhi*), as its position just before it in the Eightfold Path indicates ; not, moreover, momentary *samādhi*, to be achieved only in immobile trance-like meditation, but stillness and silence of mind as a *state of mind*—a state of mind preserved and maintained throughout the activities of life. In this state, the flow of thinking having stopped, one is "rid of outflow" (*āsavakkhina*). Thus the practice should be continued from the first establishment of waking consciousness, when the sensations of touch under the weight of one's body on the bed should immediately be noted as "Feeling", the intention to get up as "Intending" moving the arm to push back the coverlet as "Moving"—and so on. This sort of pattern should be done, so far as possible, *always* and with *all* actions—washing one's face or feeding it, chewing one's food or evacuating it, brushing one's teeth or putting them in their beaker for the night. In seeing something "Seeing", in hearing something "Hearing", in smelling "Smelling", in tasting "Tasting", in feeling a physical sensation "Feeling", in thinking "Thinking", in anger "Anger", in desire "Wanting", in amusement "Laughing"—and so on (*constant self-recollection*).

This may seem to many too strait and hard a practice, but it leads to the Pearl of Great Price—and in the end there is no other way. As one heathen philosopher has put it, "For a single bit of money sometimes there is shameful contention ; for a vain matter and slight promise men fear not to toil day and night. But, alas, for an unchangeable good, for an inestimable reward, for the highest honour, and glory without end, they grudge even the least fatigue". (From *The Imitation of Christ*). It leads, moreover, here and now to great peace and happiness—but one must pay one's tanner (of effort) first.

Since, in so far as is possible, all actions should be done recollectedly—including, with practice, such things as reading, writing, talking and listening to others—it is not possible to describe in detail how to go about each. But the pattern should already be clear.

Let us take one further example, however—that of eating. Sitting at the table the impulse will come to start eating by taking up the knife and fork. If this impulse is seen, it should be noted as "Intending" If not seen, it will probably have flown straight into a "blind" unrecollected picking up of the knife and fork. Then the impulse to actually start—"Intending" ; taking a fork-load, "Taking" ; lifting it to the mouth (slowly), "Lifting, lifting . . ." ; touching the lips, "Touching" ; taking the mouthful, "Taking" ; chewing, "Chewing" ; tasting the flavour of the food, "Tasting" ; swallowing, "Swallowing" ; taking a new fork-load, "Taking"—and so on. Taking up the teaspoon to stir one's tea, "Taking" ; moving it so as to stir, "Moving" ; stirring, "Stirring, stirring . . ." ; replacing the spoon, "Putting" ; and so on. When thoughts or noises are noticed, "Thinking" or "Hearing", and then the mind should revert to the actions. Between such actions the mind can rest on such constant stimuli as the feeling of the pressure where one is sitting, the noise of the wind, or traffic, the breath, and so on. Far from being a "distraction" such noises as motor-traffic, aircraft, the ticking of a clock, and the like, become a very satisfactory object of meditation.

Additional Breathing Exercise

After some time, as the mind becomes calmer, it will usually be found that a break occurs between breaths, normally at the end of an out-breath, before taking the new in-breath. At this unexpected halt in the proceedings, the mind is liable to hesitate, finding itself with no object, and has a tendency to wander as a result. Therefore, when this break occurs, the mind should be allowed to note one or two of the sensations always present in the body. For example, it should note the general position and feel of the body as a whole, sitting quietly at the practice. This should be noted as "Sitting". Then the feeling of pressure under the buttocks or the pressure on the ankle, if one is sitting cross-legged, should be noted as "Feeling".

In this way one, two or more points of noting should be taken to comfortably fill the gap in the breath. These notings should be done at a natural, comfortable speed, without either over-hurrying them or deliberately noting them too slowly, which will provoke distracting thoughts. The best way is to take the most prominent sensations, or if there is something in the nature of a constant noise for a time—like a passing car or aeroplane—these may be noted as "Hearing", together with the other points of sensation before the mind reverts back to the breathing at the start of the next breath. Thus, however long the pause may be in the breathing one just continues to fill it by noting such points of sensation. Sometimes the pause may be quite long—even several minutes at a later stage—in which case one just takes a round of the prominent sensations, noting them in turn, and passing on until the next breath, naturally, and of itself, starts again. For this purpose, a number of three to five points of prominent sensations to note are usually quite sufficient.

No one will pretend that the practice of Recollection during everyday life is easy—particularly in modern big-city conditions. It takes considerable and sustained effort to hold the mind at the necessary height of awareness and to withstand the constant centrifugal force around and in oneself. It is an effort which perhaps not all are prepared to attempt. Yet the alternatives are scarcely less hard, life being what it is. Without the heightened awareness and self-mastery that Recollection brings, life degenerates into a blind stumbling over the rough ground of changing circumstances that the flow of karma lays before one's feet. Man's evolution must be upwards towards greater self-awareness and self-recollection. "Evolve or die", is said to be the dictum of nature, and certainly man without Recollection is living a living death, keeping with phantoms an unprofitable strife. The Buddha has said "The recollected do not die ; the careless are as if already dead". It would be pleasanter to be able to sit back, lazily, and take it easy in life, but this turns out to be a pipe-dream ; and our minds will not let us rest—not until we have won the "victory of life"—that over Ignorance and Craving. We want to be at ease and "free", but whether this is possible depends on what we want to be free from—and for what. If we want to be free from self-discipline so as to "enjoy" the objects of the senses, this merely shows that really we are the slaves of the senses—and the intellect is a sense amongst the others. If on the other hand, we wish to be free from bondage to the senses so as to achieve self-mastery and self-realisation, this is the true freedom, and is possible to gain. This is peace, truth, life more abundant, joy and freedom.

The practice of Recollection in everyday life tends to seem more difficult than it is for two principal reasons. Firstly, one is not used to it, one has not got the hang of it, and therefore the moment one starts enthusiastically to try to practise a greater degree of Recollection in life, one finds that before very long the good impulse peters out in the face of the world's lack of co-operation, and one is back apparently just where one started. This can be greatly countered if one has once really tasted the way it feels to be truly recollected—for instance, during a period of full-time Recollection under instruction in a meditation centre. The effects of this, particularly if periodically refreshed, help to keep up the momentum.

Even so one must expect, and take in one's stride, times of apparent complete failure of Recollection. The important thing is not to let oneself be discouraged, but to pick up again. There is a saying that "the English lose all the battles except the last one". This is hardly true historically, but it is something that could perhaps be said spiritually, of the holiest of men.

The other reason that we seem to make little headway, in spite of our efforts to practise Recollection, is due to the inveterate human habit of trying to have one's cake and eat it. The "Holy Life", whether in or out of a robe, demands renunciation, a turning away from the world—that is, from the senses. This is not a running away from them, nor a rejection of them, but a lack of interest in them. As is said in the "refrain" of the Discourse on the Practice of Recollection, "abandoning desire and aversion for the world". This "Holy Indifference" is the sure entrance to proper recollection. With it, nothing would distract one, as nothing could capture our interest, neither sensual thoughts, irritations, doubts, nor all the other host of petty thoughts and memories that constantly invade the mind.

This emotional withdrawal, the renunciation of interest in conditioned things, will by no means interfere with one's ability to fulfil one's necessary function in life. On the contrary, the peace and clarity of vision brings a far greater efficiency through the joy and freedom of the knowledge that "I am not the doer".

No practice is as well suited for application in everyday life as the Practice of Recollection. It is a practice that can, and should be practised at all times and in all the varied circumstances. It is said that just as salt suits all stews, so Recollection is fitting in all events. There is the famous Zen story of the master who was asked how one should live and replied, "When hungry one eats, when tired one rests". To which the reply was "But that is how everyone lives !" "Not at all", he answered, "most people when they are eating are not just eating, they are indulging in all sorts of imaginations and idle thoughts". This is the difference between living with and without Recollection.

People often object, "But I haven't got the time to practise meditation ! I'm a busy man". No time to be more aware ? This is a strange assertion ! People have a fear that the practice of Recollection during work will interfere with the work—which really is the contrary of the truth.

Let us look, however, at the enormous amount of time being "wasted" daily. Getting up and dressing—what is one thinking of ? Washing and shaving—what is one thinking of ? Cooking breakfast— what is one thinking of ? Is it really more "efficient" to let the mind run here and there over politics, fashions, love-affairs, anxieties—than to concentrate it recollectedly on the job in hand ? Even conversing, one can be *with it*, listening when one is listening, speaking when one is speaking. Walking to the bus or underground—what is one thinking ? What is one thinking of sitting in the train ? Is it so valuable to gaze at the advertisements and the people around one ? Doing the housework—what is one thinking of ? One can be sweeping when one is sweeping, dusting when one is dusting, washing when one is washing—and so on.

Let Things Take Their Own Course

People have an almost instinctive fear that unless they "think" and "keep a grip on things" they will forget something important, and things will go wrong. In reality, though, not a quarter of the thoughts that flit through such preoccupied minds are real functional thoughts—the rest is "grasshoppering". If conditions are such that a certain action must be undertaken, years of conditioning will also ensure that the impulse occurs, and the best way not to miss it or crowd it out is to be quiet and recollected, otherwise it is more likely to be jammed out or obscured by the flow of memories, hopes, worries, and preoccupations.

To trust in the Law of Karma, the Law of Conditioning, to see that things take place as they should, secure in the realisation "It is acting through me ; I am only the instrument", is a far happier, and more recollected way of living. But of course the strength of attachments and the veil of mistaken feeling that "I am acting" cause the flow of thoughts in the usual undisciplined and harassing form.

Greater Recollection brings peace, freedom from wrong emotions, clearer judgment, and a real feeling of well-being. It kills the two great giants, Craving (*tanhā*) and Ignorance (*avijjā*), that inhabit the tangled jungle of our minds—Craving by peace and freedom from anxiety and harmful emotions, leaving joy, goodwill, compassion and the like, which do not blind the mind ; and Ignorance by clarity of vision and a growing awareness of the truth of non-self (*anattā*). "This is not mine.   This is not what I am.   This is not my true nature". In other words, "These objects have nothing to do with *me*. In no way do they touch my true being, and *I* am not the doer of these actions".   It is Ignorance that makes us identify ourselves with " our" actions, and take the responsibility for them on our shoulders.   It is thus that we tie ourselves to the Wheel of Conditioning.

Constant recollection with wisdom cuts us free—or rather shows us that we were never bound, except in THOUGHT.

May all beings be happy.